DOVER · THRIFT · EDITIONS

Selected Poems
CLAUDE McKAY

EDITED AND WITH AN INTRODUCTION BY

JOAN R. SHERMAN

DOVER PUBLICATIONS, INC.
Mineola, New York

DOVER THRIFT EDITIONS

GENERAL EDITOR: PAUL NEGRI
EDITOR OF THIS VOLUME: JOAN R. SHERMAN

Bibliographical Note

This Dover edition, first published in 1999, is a new selection of Claude McKay's poetry reprinted from standard texts. The introduction has been specially prepared for this edition.

Library of Congress Cataloging-in-Publication Data

McKay, Claude, 1890–1948.
    [Poems. Selections]
    Selected poems / Claude McKay : edited and with an introduction by Joan R. Sherman.
        p.   cm. — (Dover thrift editions)
    Includes bibliographical references and index.
    ISBN 0-486-40876-0
    1. Jamaican Americans Poetry.   2. Jamaica Poetry.   I. Sherman, Joan R. II. Title.   III. Series.
PS3525.A24785A6   1999
811'.52—dc21   99-25505
                                                                                                      CIP

Manufactured in the United States of America
Dover Publications, Inc., 31 East 2nd Street, Mineola, N.Y. 11501

Contents

From *Harlem Shadows*

(The poems below marked with an asterisk were previously published in *Spring in New Hampshire and Other Poems*. For poems originally published in periodicals, the place and date of publication are included parenthetically.)

Contents

Introduction

IN SEPTEMBER, 1918, *Pearson's Magazine* published five poems by
Claude McKay introduced by the poet's autobiographical essay, "A
Negro Poet Writes." The essay details events of McKay's life to 1918,
while it reveals his feelings for his family in Jamaica, for education and
great books, and his hatred of racism.

I am a black man, born in Jamaica, B.W.I., and have been living in
America for the last six years. During my first year's residence in America
I wrote the following group of poems. It was the first time I had ever
come face to face with such manifest, implacable hate of my race, and
my feelings were indescribable. I sent them so you may see what my
state of mind was at the time. I have written nothing similar to them
since and don't think I ever shall again.

The whites at home constitute about 14% of the population only and
they generally conform to the standard of English respectability. The
few poor ones accept their fate resignedly and live at peace with the na-
tives. The government is tolerant, somewhat benevolent, based on the
principle of equal justice to all. I had heard of prejudice in America but
never dreamed of it being so intensely bitter; for at home there is also
prejudice of the English sort, subtle and dignified, rooted in class dis-
tinction—color and race being hardly taken into account.

It was such an atmosphere I left for America to find here strong white
men, splendid types, of better physique than any I had ever seen, ex-
hibiting the most primitive animal hatred towards their weaker black
brothers. In the South daily murders of a nature most hideous and re-
volting, in the North silent acquiescence, deep hate half-hidden under
a puritan respectability, oft flaming up into an occasional lynching—
this ugly raw sore in the body of a great nation. At first I was horrified,
my spirit revolted against the ignoble cruelty and blindness of it all.
Then I soon found myself hating in return but this feeling couldn't last
long for to hate is to be miserable.

Looking about me with bigger and clearer eyes I saw that this cruelty in different ways was going on all over the world. Whites were exploiting and oppressing whites even as they exploited and oppressed the yellows and blacks. And the oppressed, groaning under the lash, evinced the same despicable hate and harshness toward their weaker fellows. I ceased to think of people and things in the mass—why should I fight with mad dogs only to be bitten and probably transformed into a mad dog myself? I turned to the individual soul, the spiritual leaders, for comfort and consolation. I felt and still feel that one must seek for the noblest and best in the individual life only: each soul must save itself.

And now this great catastrophe [World War I] has come upon the world proving the real hollowness of nationhood, patriotism, racial pride and most of the things which one was taught to respect and reverence.

There is very little to tell of my uneventful career. I was born in the heart of the little island of Jamaica on the 15th of September, 1889. My grandparents were slaves, my parents free-born. My mother was very sweet-natured, fond of books; my father, honest, stern even to harshness, hard working, beginning empty-handed he coaxed a good living from the soil, bought land, and grew to be a comparatively prosperous small settler. A firm believer in education, he tried to give all his eight children the best he could afford.

I was the last child and when I was nine years old my mother sent me to my eldest brother who was a schoolmaster in the northwestern part of the island.

From that time on I became interested in books. The school building, to which was attached the teacher's cottage, was an old slave house, plain, substantial and comfortable. My brother, an amateur journalist, country correspondent for the city papers, was fond of good books and possessed a nice library—all the great English masters and a few translations from the ancients. Not caring very much for play and having plenty of leisure I spent nearly all my time out of school reading. I read whatever pleased my fancy, secretly scribbling in prose and verse at the same time, novels, history, Bible literature, tales in verse like Scott's I read, and nearly all Shakespeare's plays for the absorbing story interest. As yet I couldn't perceive the truths. Now, looking back, I can see that that was a great formative period in my life—a time of perfect freedom to play, read and think as I liked.

I finished elementary school with my brother and helped him to teach while studying further under him. In 1906 I passed an examination for the Government Trade Scholarship and was apprenticed to a wheelwright and cabinet maker. But I couldn't learn a trade.

At this time I began writing verses of Jamaican peasant life in Negro dialect. I met an Englishman [Walter Jekyll] who loved good books and their makers more than anything else. He opened up a new world to my view, introduced me to a greater, deeper literature—to Buddha, Schopenhauer and Goethe, Carlyle and Browning, Wilde, Carpenter, Whitman, Hugo, Verlaine, Baudelaire, Shaw and the different writers of the Rationalist Press—more than I had time to read, but nearly all my spare time I spent listening to his reading choice bits from them, discussing the greatness of their minds, and telling of their lives, which I must confess I sometimes found even more interesting than their works.

Trade proved a failure. I gave it up, joined the Jamaican Constabulary 1910–11, despised it and left. With Mr. Jekyll's help, the Englishman mentioned before, my *Songs of Jamaica* was published at this time.[1] I went home and farmed rather halfheartedly. The government was then encouraging the younger men to acquire a scientific agricultural education so that it could employ them to teach the peasantry modern ways of farming. I came to America in 1912 to study agriculture, went to Tuskegee, but not liking the semi-military, machinelike existence there, I left for the Kansas State College where I stayed two years.

In the summer of 1914 I came to New York with a friend. We opened a little restaurant among our people which also proved a failure because I didn't put all my time and energy into it.

After a while I got married, but my wife wearied of the life in six months and went back to Jamaica.[2] I hated to go back after having failed at nearly everything so I just stayed here and worked desultorily—porter, houseman, janitor, butler, waiter—anything that came handy. The life was different and fascinating and one can do menial work here and feel like a man sometimes, so I don't mind it.

I am a waiter on the railroad now. Here are a few of my poems.[3]

As a dining-car waiter on the Pennsylvania Railroad (1917–19), McKay became familiar with the African-American communities of the northeast's major cities, while he maintained a home in New York City's Harlem. He responded to post-war racial riots and mob violence with militant, race-proud poems, including the famous, "If We Must Die." With publication of such fiery protest verse, mainly in Max Eastman's radical *Liberator*, McKay by the age of thirty had committed himself to left-wing political activism and to a literary career as poet, novelist, journalist, and essayist.

For fifteen years (1919–34), McKay traveled and lived in Europe—Holland, Belgium, England, France, Spain (and Morocco)—establishing his literary reputation and working at times as a model and in

---

[1] In 1912, both *Songs of Jamaica* (fifty poems) and *Constab Ballads* (twenty-eight poems) were published.

[2] In Jamaica, his wife, Eulalie Imelda Edwards, gave birth to their daughter, Rhue Hope, whom McKay would never see. His primary sexual relationships in America and Europe were homosexual.

[3] Two of these, "To the White Fiends" and "Harlem Shadows," are included below (pp. 23 and 34, respectively). McKay wrote many more poems on racial themes in 1919–23.

film studios. He went to Russia with Max Eastman in 1922–23; there the newly-empowered Communists welcomed and celebrated McKay and his art, but the poet's enthusiasm for Communism weakened as the twenties progressed. In Spain in 1928, McKay discovered that there is "a Catholic way of salvation, . . . [and] a Catholic way of life." He was inspired to study Catholicism a few years after he returned from Europe to make Harlem his home, and he ultimately became a Catholic in 1944.

McKay spent his last thirteen years in America (1934–48) writing and publishing book reviews, articles, reminiscences in which he repudiated Communism (1937), and a book of essays on Harlem and its leaders (1940). In the early 1940s, McKay fell ill, and his health steadily deteriorated. Nevertheless, he traveled to Chicago in 1944 and taught for a while in Catholic schools. He died in Chicago on May 22, 1948.

In all, McKay wrote about 200 poems. In the two collections from 1912, he portrays and celebrates the impoverished black Jamaican peasant, whose strength, pride, and superior wisdom are rooted in his native soil. McKay was the first poet to use Jamaican dialect, and his dialect is richly authentic, rhythmical, and vividly realistic in its evocation of Jamaican folksongs and peasant life. The poet's love for and identification with Jamaica's landscape and nature's beauties characterizes poems throughout his career and often contrasts with hatred for the city. The city, from Kingston to New York, symbolizes corruption and evil, racial oppression and social injustice. McKay's "American" poems, written after 1912, are admirable for their disciplined craftsmanship, depth of feeling, solid roots in the natural Jamaican world, and universally valid spiritual values. These poems, which greatly influenced the burst of black creativity known as the Harlem Renaissance, include angry denunciations of the white world's discriminatory practices; nostalgic hymns to the easygoing tropical life and joys of nature; love poems; and expressions of McKay's spiritual quest for truth.

Works by Claude McKay

Poetry
Songs of Jamaica. Kingston, Jamaica: Aston W. Gardner, 1912.
Constab Ballads. London: Watts, 1912.
Spring in New Hampshire and Other Poems. London: Grant Richards, 1920.
Harlem Shadows. New York: Harcourt, Brace, 1922.
Selected Poems of Claude McKay. New York: Bookman Associates, 1953.

Novels
Home to Harlem. New York: Harper and Bros., 1928.
Banjo: A Story Without a Plot. New York: Harper and Bros., 1929.
Banana Bottom. New York: Harper and Bros., 1933.

Autobiography
A Long Way from Home. New York: Lee Furman, 1937.

Short Stories
Gingertown. New York: Harper and Bros., 1932.

Collected Essays
Harlem: Negro Metropolis. New York: E. P. Dutton, 1940.

Songs of Jamaica

QUASHIE TO BUCCRA*

You tas'e petater an' you say it sweet,
But you no know how hard we wuk fe it;
You want a basketful fe quattiewut,
'Cause you no know how 'tiff de bush fe cut.

De cowitch under which we hab fe 'toop,
De shamar lyin' t'ick like pumpkin soup,
Is killin' somet'ing for a naygur man;
Much less de cutlass workin' in we han'.

De sun hot like when fire ketch a town;
Shade-tree look temptin', yet we caan' lie down,
Aldough we wouldn' eben ef we could,
Causen we job must finish soon an' good.

De bush cut done, de bank dem we deh dig,
But dem caan' 'tan' sake o' we naybor pig;
For so we moul' it up he root it do'n,
An' we caan' 'peak sake o' we naybor tongue.

Aldough de vine is little, it can bear;
It wantin' not'in' but a little care:
You see petater tear up groun', you run,
You laughin', sir, you must be t'ink a fun.

De fiel' pretty? It couldn't less 'an dat,
We wuk de bes', an' den de lan' is fat;
We dig de row dem eben in a line,
An' keep it clean—den so it *mus'* look fine.

---

*"Quashie" (and "naygur," line 7) is the black man who speaks to "Buccra," the white
man (Ed.).

1

You tas'e petater an' you say it sweet,
But you no know how hard we wuk fe it;
Yet still de hardship always melt away
Wheneber it come roun' to reapin' day.

HARD TIMES

De mo' me wuk, de mo' time hard,
   I don't know what fe do;
I ben' me knee an' pray to Gahd,
   Yet t'ings same as befo'.

De taxes knockin' at me door,
   I hear de bailiff's v'ice;
Me wife is sick, can't get no cure,
   But gnawin' me like mice.

De picknies hab to go to school
   Widout a bite fe taste;
And I am working like a mule,
While buccra, sittin' in de cool,
   Hab 'nuff nenyam fe waste.

De clodes is tearin' off dem back
   When money seems noa mek;
A man can't eben ketch a mac,
   Care how him 'train him neck.

De peas won't pop, de corn can't grow,
   Poor people face look sad;
Dat Gahd would cuss de lan' I'd know,
   For black naygur too bad.

I won't gib up, I won't say die,
   For all de time is hard;
Aldough de wul' soon en', I'll try
My wutless best as time goes by,
   An' trust on in me Gahd.

CUDJOE FRESH FROM DE LECTURE

'Top *one* minute, Cous' Jarge, an' sit do'n 'pon de grass,
An' mek a tell you 'bout de news I hear at las',
How de buccra te-day tek time an' bégin teach
All of us dat was deh in a clear open speech.

You miss somet'ing fe true, but a wi' mek you know,
As much as how a can, how de business a go:
Him tell us 'bout we self, an' mek we fresh again,
An' talk about de wul' from commencement to en'.

Me look 'pon me black 'kin, an' so me head grow big,
Aldough me heaby han' dem hab fe plug an' dig;
For ebery single man, no car' about dem rank,
Him bring us ebery one an' put 'pon de same plank.

Say, parson do de same? Yes, in a diff'ren' way,
For parson tell us how de whole o' we are clay;
An' lookin' close at t'ings, we hab to pray quite hard
Fe swaller wha' him say an' don't t'ink bad o' Gahd.

But dis man tell us 'traight 'bout how de whole t'ing came,
An' show us widout doubt how Gahd was not fe blame;
How change cause eberyt'ing fe mix up 'pon de eart',
An' dat most hardship come t'rough accident o' birt'.

Him show us all a sort o' funny 'keleton,
Wid names I won't remember under dis ya sun;
Animals queer to deat', dem bone, teet', an' head-skull,
All dem so dat did live in a de ole-time wul'.

No 'cos say we get cuss mek fe we 'kin come so,
But fe all t'ings come 'quare, same so it was to go:
Seems our lan' must ha' been a bery low-do'n place,
Mek it tek such long time in tu'ning out a race.

Yes, from monkey we spring: I believe ebery wud;
It long time better dan f'go say we come from mud:
No need me keep back part, me hab not'in' fe gain;
It's ebery man dat born—de buccra mek it plain.

It really strange how some o' de lan' dem advance;
Man power in some ways is nummo soso chance;
But suppose eberyt'ing could tu'n right upside down,
Den p'raps we'd be on top an' givin' some one houn'.

Yes, Cous' Jarge, slabery hot fe dem dat gone befo':
We gettin' better times, for those days we no know;
But I t'ink it do good, tek we from Africa
An' lan' us in a blessed place as dis a ya.

Talk 'bouten Africa, we would be deh till now,
Maybe same half-naked—all day dribe buccra cow,
An' tearin' t'rough de bush wid all de monkey dem,
Wile an' uncibilise', an' neber comin' tame.

A MIDNIGHT WOMAN TO THE BOBBY

No palm me up, you dutty brute,
You' jam mout' mash like ripe bread-fruit;
You fas'n now, but wait lee ya,
I'll see you grunt under de law.

You t'ink you wise, but we wi' see;
You not de fus' one fas' wid me;
I'll lib fe see dem tu'n you out,
As sure as you got dat mash' mout'.

I born right do'n beneat' de clack
(You ugly brute, you tu'n you' back?)
Don' t'ink dat I'm a come-aroun',
I born right 'way in 'panish Town.

Care how you try, you caan' do mo'
Dan many dat was hyah befo';
Yet whe' dey all o' dem te-day?
De buccra dem no kick dem 'way?

Ko 'pon you' jam samplatta nose:
'Cos you wear Mis'r Koshaw clo'es
You t'ink say you's de only man,
Yet fus' time ko how you be'n 'tan'.

You big an' ugly ole tu'n-foot
Be'n neber know fe wear a boot;

An' chigger nyam you' tumpa toe,
Till nit full i' like herrin' roe.

You come from mountain naked-'kin,
An' Lard a mussy! you be'n thin,
For all de bread-fruit dem be'n done,
Bein' 'poil' up by de tearin' sun:

I lef' quite 'way from wha' we be'n deh talk about,
Yet still a couldn' help—de wuds come to me mout';
Just like how yeas' get strong an' sometimes fly de cark,
Same way me feelings grow, so I was boun' fe talk.

Yet both horse partly runnin' in de selfsame gallop,
For it is nearly so de way de buccra pull up:
Him say, how de wul' stan', dat right will neber be,
But wrong will eber gwon till dis wul' en' fe we.

MY NATIVE LAND, MY HOME

Dere is no land dat can compare
    Wid you where'er I roam;
In all de wul' none like you fair,
    My native land, my home.

Jamaica is de nigger's place,
    No mind whe' some declare;
Although dem call we "no-land race,"
    I know we home is here.

You give me life an' nourishment,
    No udder land I know;
My lub I neber can repent,
    For all to you I owe.

E'en ef you mek me beggar die,
    I'll trust you all de same,
An' none de less on you rely,
    Nor saddle you wid blame.

Though you may cas' me from your breas'
    An' trample me to deat',
My heart will trus' you none de less,
    My land I won't feget.

An' I hope none o' your sons would
   Refuse deir strengt' to lend,
An' drain de last drop o' deir blood
   Their country to defend.

You draw de t'ousan' from deir shore,
   An' all 'long keep dem please';
De invalid come here fe cure,
   You heal all deir disease.

Your fertile soil grow all o' t'ings
   To full de naygur's wants,
'Tis seamed wid neber-failing springs
   To give dew to de plants.

You hab all t'ings fe mek life bles',
   But buccra 'poil de whole
Wid gove'mint an' all de res',
   Fe worry naygur soul.

Still all dem little chupidness
   Caan' tek away me lub;
De time when I'll tu'n 'gains' you is
   When you can't give me grub.

MY MOUNTAIN HOME

De mango tree in yellow bloom,
   De pretty akee seed,
De mammee where de John-to-whits come
   To have their daily feed,

Show you de place where I was born,
   Of which I am so proud,
'Mongst de banana-field an' corn
   On a lone mountain-road.

One Sunday marnin' 'fo' de hour
   Fe service-time come on,
Ma say dat I be'n born to her
   Her little las'y son.

Those early days be'n neber dull,
   My heart was ebergreen;

How I did lub my little wul'
   Surrounded by pingwin!

An' growin' up, with sweet freedom
   About de yard I'd run;
An' tired out I'd hide me from
   De fierce heat of de sun.

So glad I was de fus' day when
   Ma sent me to de spring;
I was so happy feelin' then
   Dat I could do somet'ing.

De early days pass quickly 'long,
   Soon I became a man,
An' one day found myself among
   Strange folks in a strange lan'.

My little joys, my wholesome min',
   Dey bullied out o' me,
And made me daily mourn an' pine
   An' wish dat I was free.

Dey taught me to distrust my life,
   Dey taught me what was grief;
For months I travailed in de strife,
   'Fo' I could find relief.

But I'll return again, my Will,
   An' where my wild ferns grow
An' weep for me on Dawkin's Hill,
   Dere, Willie, I shall go.

An' dere is somet'ing near forgot,
   Although I lub it best;
It is de loved, de hallowed spot
   Where my dear mother rest.

Look good an' find it, Willie dear,
   See dat from bush 'tis free;
Remember that my heart is near,
   An' you say you lub me.

An' plant on it my fav'rite fern,
   Which I be'n usual wear;
In days to come I shall return
   To end my wand'rin's dere.

JUBBA

My Jubba waiting dere fe me;
Me, knowin', went out on de spree,
An' she, she wait deh till midnight,
Bleach-bleachin' in de cold moonlight:
An' when at last I did go home
I found out dat she had just come,
An' now she tu'n her back away,
An' won't listen a wud I say.

    Forgive me, Jubba, Jubba dear,
      As you are standing, standing there,
      An' I will no more mek you grieve,
      My Jubba, ef you'll but forgive.

I'll go to no more dancing booth,
I'll play no more wid flirty Ruth,
I didn' mean a t'ing, Jubba,
I didn' know you'd bex fe da';
I only took two set o' dance
An' at de bidding tried me chance;
I buy de big crown-bread fe you,
An' won't you tek it, Jubba?—do.

    Forgive me, Jubba, Jubba dear,
      As you are standing, standing there,
      An' I will no more mek you grieve,
      My Jubba, ef you'll but forgive.

I was a nice tea-meeting though,
None o' de boy dem wasn' slow,
An' it was pack' wid pretty gal,
So de young man was in dem sall;
But when I 'member you a yard
I know dat you would t'ink it hard,
Aldough, Jubba, 'twas sake o' spite
Mek say you wouldn' come te-night.

    Forgive me, Jubba, Jubba dear,
      As you are standing, standing there,
      An' I will no more mek you grieve,
      My Jubba, ef you'll but forgive.

I lef' you, Jub, in such a state,
I neber knew dat you would wait;
Yet all de while I couldn' res',
De t'ought o' you was in me breas';
So nummo time I couldn' was'e,
But me go get me pillow-case
An' put in deh you bread an' cake—
Forgive me, Jubba, fe God sake!

Forgive me, Jubba, Jubba dear,
As you are standing, standing there,
An' I will no more mek you grieve,
My Jubba, ef you'll but forgive.

Constab Ballads

PREFACE

LET me confess it at once. I had not in me the stuff that goes to the making of a good constable; for I am so constituted that imagination outruns discretion, and it is my misfortune to have a most improper sympathy with wrongdoers. I therefore never "made cases," but turning, like Nelson, a blind eye to what it was my manifest duty to see, tried to make peace, which seemed to me better.

Moreover, I am, by temperament, unadaptive; by which I mean that it is not in me to conform cheerfully to uncongenial usages. We blacks are all somewhat impatient of discipline, and to the natural impatience of my race there was added, in my particular case, a peculiar sensitiveness which made certain forms of discipline irksome, and a fierce hatred of injustice. Not that I ever openly rebelled; but the rebellion was in my heart, and it was fomented by the inevitable rubs of daily life—trifles to most of my comrades, but to me calamities and tragedies. To relieve my feelings, I wrote poems, and into them I poured my heart in its various moods. This volume consists of a selection from these poems.

The life was, as it happened, unsuited to me, and I to it; but I do not regret my experiences. If I had enemies whom I hated, I also had close friends whom I loved.

One word in conclusion. As constituted by the authorities the Force is admirable, and it only remains for the men themselves, and especially the sub-officers, to make it what it should be, a harmonious band of brothers.

C. McK.

BENNIE'S DEPARTURE

All dat week was cold an' dreary,
  An' I worked wid heavy heart;
All my limbs were weak an' weary,
  When I knew that we would part;
An' I thought of our first meeting
  On dat pleasant day o' June,
Of his kind an' modest greeting
  When we met dat afternoon;

Of de cáprice o' de weader,
  How de harsh rain fell dat day,
How we kissed de book togeder,
  An' our hearts were light an' gay;
How we started homewards drivin',
  Last civilian drive in train;
How we half-feared de arrivin',
  Knowin' we were not free again;

How we feared do'n to de layin'
  By of our loved old-time dress,
An' to each udder kept sayin'
  All might be unhappiness;
How our lives be'n full o' gladness,
  Drillin' wid hearts light an' free;
How for days all would be sadness
  When we quarrelled foolishly.

An' de sad, glad recollection
  Brought a strange thrill to my soul,
'Memberin' how his affection
  Gave joy in a barren wul':
As I thought then, my mind goin'
  Back to mem'ries, oh! so dear,—
As I felt de burden growin',
  Jes' so shall I write it here.

We were once more on de drill-ground,
  Me so happy by his side,
One in passion, one in will, bound
  By a boundless love an' wide:

Daily you would see us drinkin'
   Our tea by de mess-room door,
Every passin' moment linkin'
   Us togeder more an' more.

After little lazy leanin',
   Sittin' on de window-sill,
Me would start our carbine-cleanin'
   For de eight o'clock big drill:
'Fo' me he be'n always ready,
   An' as smart as smart could be;
He was always quick, yet steady,
   Not of wav'rin' min' like me.

When de time was awful dull in
   De ole borin' Depôt-school,
An' me face was changed an' sullen,
   An' I kicked against de rule,
He would speak to me so sweetly,
   Tellin' me to bear my fate,
An' his lovin' words completely
   Helped me to forget de hate.

An' my heart would start a-pinin'
   Ef, when one o'clock came roun',
He was not beside me dinin',
   But be'n at some duty boun':
Not a t'ing could sweet me eatin',
   Wid my Bennie 'way from me;
Strangely would my heart be beatin'
   Tell I knew dat he was free.

When at last he came to table,
   Neider one could ever bate
Tell in some way we were able
   To eke out each udder plate:
All me t'oughts were of my frennie
   Then an' in de after days;
Ne'er can I forget my Bennie
   Wid him nice an' pleasant ways.

In de evenin' we went walkin',
   An' de sweet sound of his voice,
As we laughed or kept a-talkin',

Made my lovin' heart rejoice:
Full of happiness we strolled on,
   In de closin' evenin' light,
Where de stately Cobre rolled on
   Gurglin', murm'rin' in de night;

Claspin' of our hands togeder,
   Each to each we told good-night,
Dreamed soon o' life's broken ledder
   An' de wul's perplexin' fight,
Of de many souls a-weepin'
   Burdened do'n wid care an' strife,
While we sweetly lay a-sleepin',
   Yet would grumble 'bout our life.

Once his cot was next beside me,
   But dere came misfortune's day
When de pleasure was denied me,
   For de sergeant moved him 'way:
I played not fe mind de movin'
   Though me heart wid grief be'n full;
'Twas but one kin' o' de provin'
   O' de ways o' dis ya wul'.

'Fo' we tu'n good, came de warnin'
   O' de rousin' bugle-soun',
An' you'd see us soon a marnin'
   To de bat'-house hurryin' down,
Leavin' udders yawnin', fumblin',
   Wid deir limbs all stiff an' ole,
Or 'pon stretchin' out an' grumblin',
   Say'n' de water be'n too col'.

In a jiffy we were washin',
   Jeerin' dem, de lazy type,
All about us water dashin'
   Out o' de ole-fashion' pipe:
In a lee while we were endin',—
   Dere was not much time to kill,—
Arms an' bay'nets wanted tendin'
   'Fo' de soon-a-marnin' drill.

So we spent five months togeder,
   He was ever staunch an' true

In sunshine or rainy weader,
   No mind what wrong I would do:
But dere came de sad heart-rendin'
   News dat he must part from me,
An' I nursed my sorrow, bendin'
   To de grim necessity.

All dat week was cold an' dreary,
   An' I worked wid heavy heart;
All my limbs were weak an' weary
   When I knew dat we would part;
All de fond hopes, all de gladness
   Drooped an' faded from our sight,
An' an overwhelmin' sadness
   Came do'n on de partin' night.

In de dim light I lay thinkin'
   How dat sad night was our last,
My lone spirit weakly sinkin'
   'Neat' de mem'ries o' de past:
As I thought in deepest sorrow,
   He came,—sat do'n by my side,
Speakin' o' de dreaded morrow
   An' de flow o' life's dark tide.

Gently fell the moonbeams, kissin'
   'Way de hot tears streamin' free,
While de wind outside went hissin'
   An' a-moanin' for poor me:
Then he rose, but after bended,
   Biddin' me a last good-bye;
To his cot his steps he wended,
   An' I heard a deep-drawn sigh.

'Twas de same decisive warnin'
   Wakin' us as in de past,
An' we both washed soon a marnin'
   'Neat' de ole pipe fe de last;
We be'n filled wid hollow laughter,
   Rather tryin' to take heart,
But de grief returned when after
   Came de moment fe depart.

Hands gripped tight, but not a tear fell
   As I looked into his face,
Said de final word o' farewell,
   An' returned back to my place:
At my desk I sat me dry-eyed,
   Sometimes gave a low-do'n moan,
An' at moments came a sigh sighed
   For my Bennie dat was gone.

Gone he, de little sunshine o' my life,
Leavin' me 'lone to de Depôt's black strife,
Dear little comrade o' lecture an' drill,
Loved comrade, like me of true stubborn will:
Oft, in de light o' de fast sinkin' sun,
We'd frolic togeder aroun' de big gun;
Oft would he laughingly run after me,
Chasin' me over de wide Depôt lea;
Oft would he teach me de folly o' pride
When, me half-vexed, he would sit by my side;—
Now all is blackness t'rough night an' t'rough day,
For my heart's weary now Bennie's away.

CONSOLATION

I took my marnin' bat' alone,
An' wept for Bennie dat was gone;
An' after,—sittin', weepin' long,—
Some one came askin' wha' be'n wrong:
But only chokin' sobs he heard,
My mout' could never speak a word.
An' so for long days all was grief,
An' never could I get relief;
My heart be'n full of emptiness,
With naught to love an' naught to bless.

I 'member de familiar scene:—
I sat out on de Depôt green,
Restin' agains' de big great gun:
De long rays o' de settin' sun
Were thrown upon the sombre wall;

I heard de rousin' bugle-call
In chorus soundin' o' retreat;
A ray o' light shone on my seat,
A soft dull shade of changin' gold,
So pleasant, lovely to behold:
A moment,—an' I was alone,
De wanin' evenin' sun was gone.

I sat do'n still; de evenin' light
Passed on, an' it fell night, dark night.
'Twas autumn: feelin' rather chill,
I rose, led by my aimless will,
An' went up to the second floor,
Sat on a bench agains' de door.
A comrade came an' sat by me,
Restin' a hand upon my knee;
De lantern old was burnin' dim,
But bright 'nough for me to see him:—
One searchin' look into his face,
I gave him in my heart a place.

I never knew a nicer mind,
He was so pleasant an' so kind;
An' oh! the sweetness of his voice
That made my lonely heart rejoice.
It all comes back so vividly,—
The comfort that he brought to me;
The ray of hope, the pure pure joy
He gave a poor forsaken boy;
In walk or talk his tender care,
His deep concern for my welfare.
His comin' filled the larger part
Of de great void made in my heart
When on dat cruel awful day
My faithful Bennie went away.

'Tis not de way o' dis ya wul'
Dat any miserable soul
Should know a little lastin' peace,
Should taste endurin' happiness.
De harmless tabby o' de house
Plays kindly wid de frightened mouse,
Till, when it nearly loses dread,

Good Lard! de little thing is dead.
So wid de man, toy of a Will
E'er playin' with him to its fill,
To-day alive, to-morrow slain,—
Thus all our pleasure ends in pain.

Where'er I roam, whate'er the clime,
I'll never know a happier time;
I seemed as happy as could be,
When—everything was torn from me.
De fateful day I 'member still,
De final breakin' o' my will,
Again de sayin' o' good-bye,
My poor heart's silent wailin' cry;
My life, my soul, my all be'n gone,
And ever since I am alone.

A RECRUIT ON THE CORPY

Me an' de corpy drink we rum,
An' corpy larn me how fe bum;
Last night me gie 'm de last-last tup,
Yet now him come an' bring me up.

He'll carry me 'fo' officer,
An' rake up' t'ings fe charge me for;
An' all because dese couple days
Me couldn' gie 'm de usual raise.

Last night, when it come to roll-call,
Dis corpy couldn' 'ten' at all:
We didn' mek de S.M. see 'm,
But only put things 'traight fe him.

An' we, like big fools, be'n deh fret
Ober de corpy drunk to deat':
We all treat him so very kin',
Aldough him ha' such dutty min'.

We tek him drunken off de car,
We tek him drunken out de bar,
We wake him drunken 'pon him guard,
An' yet we neber claim reward.

All bad contráry things me do,
Corpy see me an' let me go;
But 'causen me no ha' a tup,
Fe not'in' 'tall him bring me up.

THE APPLE-WOMAN'S COMPLAINT

While me deh walk 'long in de street,
Policeman's yawnin' on his beat;
An' dis de wud him chiefta'n say—
Me mus'n' car' me apple-tray.

Ef me no wuk, me boun' fe tief;
S'pose dat will please de pólice chief!
De prison dem mus' be wan' full,
Mek dem's 'pon we like ravin' bull.

Black nigger wukin' laka cow
An' wipin' sweat-drops from him brow,
Dough him is dyin' sake o' need,
P'lice an' dem headman boun' fe feed.

P'lice an' dem headman gamble too,
Dey shuffle card an' bet fe true;
Yet ef me Charlie gamble,—well,
Dem try fe 'queeze him laka hell.

De headman fe de town police
Mind neber know a little peace,
'Cep' when him an' him heartless ban'
Hab sufferin' nigger in dem han'.

Ah son-son! dough you 're bastard, yah,
An' dere's no one you can call pa,
Jes' try to ha' you' mudder's min'
An' Police Force you'll neber jine.

But how judge bélieve pólicemen,
Dem dutty mout' wid lyin' stain'?
While we go batterin' along
Dem doin' we all sort o' wrong.

We hab fe barter-out we soul
To lib t'rough dis ungodly wul';—

O massa Jesus! don't you see
How pólice is oppressin' we?

Dem wan' fe see we in de street
Dah foller dem all 'pon dem beat;
An' after, 'dout a drop o' shame,
Say we be'n dah solicit dem.

Ah massa Jesus! in you' love
Jes' look do'n from you' t'rone above,
An' show me how a poo' weak gal
Can lib good life in dis ya wul'.

THE HEART OF A CONSTAB

'Tis hatred without an' 'tis hatred within,
    An' I am so weary an' sad;
For all t'rough de tempest o' terrible strife
    Dere's not'in' to make poor me glad.

Oh! where are de faces I loved in de past,
    De frien's dat I used to hold dear?
Oh say, have dey all turned away from me now
    Becausen de red seam I wear?

I foolishly wandered away from dem all
    To dis life of anguish an' woe,
Where I mus' be hard on me own kith an' kin,
    And even to frien' mus' prove foe.

Oh! what have I gained from my too too rash act
    O' joinin' a hard Constab Force,
Save quenchin' me thirst from a vinegar cup,
    De vinegar cup o' remorse?

I t'ought of a livin' o' pure honest toil,
    To keep up dis slow-ebbin' breath;
But no, de life surely is bendin' me do'n,
    Is bendin' me do'n to de death.

'Tis grievous to think dat, while toilin' on here,
    My people won't love me again,
My people, my people, me owna black skin,—
    De wretched t'ought gives me such pain.

But I'll leave it, my people, an' come back to you,
    I'll flee from de grief an' turmoil;
I'll leave it, though flow'rs here should line my path yet,
    An' come back to you an' de soil.

For 'tis hatred without an' 'tis hatred within,
    An' how can I live 'douten heart?
Then oh for de country, de love o' me soul,
    From which I shall nevermore part!

SUKEE RIVER

    I shall love you ever,
    Dearest Sukee River:
Dash against my broken heart,
Nevermore from you I'll part,
    But will stay forever,
    Crystal Sukee River.

    Cool my fevered brow:
    Ah! 'tis better now,
As I serpent-like lance t'rough
Your broad pool o' deepest blue!
    Dis once burnin' brow
    Is more better now.

    All about me dashin',
    H'is'in' up an' splashin',
Bubbles like de turtle-berries,
Jostlin' wid de yerry-yerries,
    All about me dashin'
    H'is'in' up an' splashin'.

    Oh! dis blissful swim,
    Like a fairy dream!
Jumpin' off de time-worn plank,
Pupperlicks from bank to bank,
    Dis delightful swim
    Is a fairy dream.

    Kiss my naked breast
    In its black skin drest:
Let your dainty silver bubbles

Ease it of its lifelong troubles,
　　Dis my naked breast
　　In its black skin drest.

Floatin', floatin' down
　　On my back alone,
Kiss me on my upturned face,
Clasp me in your fond embrace,
　　As I'm floatin' down
　　Happy, yet alone.

Wavelets laughin' hound me,
　　Ripples glad surround me:
Catchin' at dem light an' gay,
See dem scamper all away,
　　As dey playful hound me,
　　Or in love surround me.

T'rough de twistin' dance
　　Onward do I lance:
Onward under yonder cave
Comes wid me a pantin' wave,
　　Speedin' from de dance
　　Wid me as I lance.

'Neat' dis shadin' hedge
　　Growin' by your bridge,
I am thinkin' o' you' love,
Love dat not'in' can remove,
　　'Neat' dis shadin' hedge
　　Growin' by your bridge.

Love more pure, I ken,
　　Dan de love o' men,
Knowin' not de fickle mind
Nor de hatred o' my kind;
　　Purer far, I ken,
　　Dan de love o' men.

E'en when welcome deat'
　　Claims dis painful breat',
Of you I will ever think
Who first gave me crystal drink;
　　E'en when welcome deat'
　　Claims dis painful breat'.

For a little while
I must leave your smile:
Raindrops fallin' from de sky
Force me now to say good-bye;
Jes' lee bit o' while
I must leave your smile.

Foamin' Sukee River,
Dearer now dan ever,
I'll ne'er roam from you again
To a life o' so-so pain,
Crystal flowin' river,
Dearer now dan ever.

Uncollected Poems

INVOCATION

Ancestral Spirit, hidden from my sight
By modern Time's unnumbered works and ways
On which in awe and wonderment I gaze,
Where hid'st thou in the deepness of the night?
What evil powers thy healing presence blight?
Thou who from out the dark and dust didst raise
The Ethiop standard in the curtained days,
Before the white God said: Let there be light!
Bring ancient music to my modern heart,
Let fall the light upon my sable face
That once gleamed upon the Ethiopian's art;
Lift me to thee out of this alien place
So I may be, thine exiled counterpart,
The worthy singer of my world and race.

TO THE WHITE FIENDS

Think you I am not fiend and savage too?
Think you I could not arm me with a gun
And shoot down ten of you for every one
Of my black brothers murdered, burnt by you?
Be not deceived, for every deed you do
I could match—out-match: am I not Afric's son,
Black of that black land where black deeds are done?
But the Almighty from the darkness drew

23

My soul and said: Even thou shalt be a light
Awhile to burn on the benighted earth,
Thy dusky face I set among the white
For thee to prove thyself of higher worth;
Before the world is swallowed up in night,
To show thy little lamp: go forth, go forth!

THE DOMINANT WHITE

God gave you power to build and help and lift;
    But you proved prone to persecute and slay
And from the high and noble course to drift
    Into the darkness from the light of day.
He gave you law and order, strength of will
    The lesser peoples of the world to lead;
You chose to break and crush them through life's mill,
    But for your earthly gains to make them bleed:
Because you've proved unworthy of your trust,
God—He shall humble you down to the dust.

You have betrayed the black, maligned the yellow;
    But what else could we hope of you who set
The hand even of your own against his fellow;
    To stem the dire tide that threatens yet?
You called upon the name of your false god
    To lash our wounded flesh with knotted cords
And trample us into the blood-stained sod,
    And justified your deeds with specious words:
Oh! you have proved unworthy of your trust,
And God shall humble you down to the dust.

The pain you gave us nothing can assuage,
    Who hybridized a proud and virile race,
Bequeathed to it a bastard heritage
    And made the black ashamed to see his face.
You ruined him, put doubt into his heart,
    You set a sword between him and his kin,
And preached to him, with simple, lying art
    About the higher worth of your white skin!
Oh White Man! You have trifled with your trust,
    And God shall humble you down to the dust.

You blinded go, afraid to see the Truth,
   Closing your eyes to and denying Beauty;
You stultify the dreams of visioned youth
   All in the prostituted name of Duty.
You place your Seers with madmen, fools and rogues,
   Their words distort and twist, despise their creed:
You choose instead the little demagogues
   That will uphold you in your shameless greed:
Because you've proved unworthy of your trust,
Oh, He shall humble you!—down to the dust.

A CAPITALIST AT DINNER

An ugly figure, heavy, overfed,
  —Settles uneasily into a chair;
Nervously he mops his pimply pink bald head,
Frowns at the fawning waiter standing near.
The entire service tries its best to please
This overpampered piece of broken-health,
Who sits there thoughtless, querulous, obese,
Wrapped in his sordid visions of vast wealth.

Great God! if creatures like this money-fool,
Who hold the service of mankind so cheap,
Over the people must forever rule,
Driving them at their will like helpless sheep—
Then let proud mothers cease from giving birth;
Let human beings perish from the earth.

THE NEGRO DANCERS

I.

Lit with cheap colored lights a basement den,
   With rows of chairs and tables on each side,
And, all about, young, dark-skinned women and men
   Drinking and smoking, merry, vacant-eyed.

A Negro band, that scarcely seems awake,
 Drones out half-heartedly a lazy tune,
While quick and willing boys their order take
 And hurry to and from the near saloon.
Then suddenly a happy, lilting note
 Is struck, the walk and hop and trot begin,
Under the smoke upon foul air afloat;
 Around the room the laughing puppets spin
  To sound of fiddle, drum and clarinet,
  Dancing, their world of shadows to forget.

II.

'Tis best to sit and gaze; my heart then dances
 To the lithe bodies gliding slowly by,
The amorous and inimitable glances
 That subtly pass from roguish eye to eye,
The laughter gay like sounding silver ringing,
 That fills the whole wide room from floor to ceiling,—
A rush of rapture to my tried soul bringing—
 The deathless spirit of a race revealing.
Not one false step, no note that rings not true!
 Unconscious even of the higher worth
Of their great art, they serpent-wise glide through
 The syncopated waltz. Dead to the earth
  And her unkindly ways of toil and strife,
  For them the dance is the true joy of life.

III.

And yet they are the outcasts of the earth,
 A race oppressed and scorned by ruling man;
How can they thus consent to joy and mirth
 Who live beneath a world-eternal ban?
No faith is theirs, no shining ray of hope,
 Except the martyr's faith, the hope that death
Some day will free them from their narrow scope
And once more merge them with the infinite breath.
But, oh! they dance with poetry in their eyes
 Whose dreamy loveliness no sorrow dims,

And parted lips and eager, gleeful cries,
   And perfect rhythm in their nimble limbs.
      The gifts divine are theirs, music and laughter;
      All other things, however great, come after.

THE LITTLE PEOPLES

The little peoples of the troubled earth,
The little nations that are weak and white;—
For them the glory of another birth.
For them the lifting of the veil of night.
The big men of the world in concert met,
Have sent forth in their power a new decree:
Upon the old harsh wrongs the sun must set,
Henceforth the little peoples must be free!

But we, the blacks, less than the trampled dust,
Who walk the new ways with the old dim eyes,—
We to the ancient gods of greed and lust
Must still be offered up as sacrifice:
Oh, we who deign to live but will not dare,
The white world's burden must forever bear!

TO "HOLY" RUSSIA

Long struggling under the Imperial heel,
Some dared not see the white flame of your star
Dimmed by the loathsome shadow of your Tsar.
But men who clung to sacred dreams could feel

Some day you would put forth your arm of steel
And drag the mannikins from near and far,
Before the mighty people's judgment bar,
To answer for the ruined commonweal . . .

Down from their high, dishonoured place you hurled
The cowed, incompetent, corrupted few;
The blood-bathed flag of a new life unfurled,

Revealed your soul alike to Slav and Jew:
The eyes of the too-long submissive world,
Lifted in golden hope, are turned to you!

SONG OF THE NEW SOLDIER AND WORKER

We are tired, tired, tired—we are work-weary and war-weary;
  What though the skies are soft-blue and the birds still sing
And the balmy air of day is like wine? Life is dreary
  And the whole wide world is sick and suffering.

We are weary, weary, weary, sad and tired and no longer
  Will we go on as before, glad to be the willing tools
Of the hard and heartless few, the favoured and the stronger,
  Who have strength to crush and kill, for we are fools.

We will calmly fold our arms sore from labouring, and aching,
  We will not still feed and guard the hungry, hideous, huge machine
That yawns with ugly mouth, performs its grim task of life-breaking
  Like a fat whore, coarse and brazen and obscene.

O, to pull the thing to pieces! O, to wreck it all and smash
  With the power and the will that only holy hate can give;
Even though our broken bodies may be caught in the crash—
  Even so—that children yet unborn may live!

BATTLE

Last night I dreamed that in the deadly strife,
Where privileged power rules with ruthless might,
I saw my body, a corpse still breathing life,
Trampled and mangled, a bloody, blackened sight.
If such should be my fate, I pray it will
Come to me sudden-swift, a keen sword-dart,
Sent deeply through my burning breast to still
The rhythmic beat of my rebellious heart.
So, I should have the grand end come to me,
While following the only way of duty
And questing for the soul of truth and beauty!
I'd go convinced that there could never be
A fairer life for truth or beauty's flower,
While earth is ruled by man's imperial power.

NEGRO SPIRITUAL

They've taken thee out of the simple soil,
Where the warm sun made mellowy thy tones,
And voices plaintive from eternal toil,
Thy music spoke in liquid lyric moans;
They've stolen thee out of the brooding wood,
Where scenting bloodhounds caught thy whispered note,
And birds and flowers only understood
The sorrow sobbing from a choking throat;
And set thee in this garish marble hall
Of faces hard with conscience-worried pride,
Like convicts witnessing a carnival,
For whom an alien vandal mind has tried
To fashion thee for virtuoso wonders,
Drowning thy beauty in orchestral thunders.

THE WHITE HOUSE

Your door is shut against my tightened face,
And I am sharp as steel with discontent;
But I possess the courage and the grace
To bear my anger proudly and unbent.
The pavement slabs burn loose beneath my feet,
A chafing savage, down the decent street;
And passion rends my vitals as I pass,
Where boldly shines your shuttered door of glass.
Oh, I must search for wisdom every hour,
Deep in my wrathful bosom sore and raw,
And find in it the superhuman power
To hold me to the letter of your law!
Oh, I must keep my heart inviolate
Against the potent poison of your hate.

*Harlem Shadows**

AMERICA

Although she feeds me bread of bitterness,
And sinks into my throat her tiger's tooth,
Stealing my breath of life, I will confess
I love this cultured hell that tests my youth!
Her vigor flows like tides into my blood,
Giving me strength erect against her hate.
Her bigness sweeps my being like a flood.
Yet as a rebel fronts a king in state,
I stand within her walls with not a shred
Of terror, malice, not a word of jeer.
Darkly I gaze into the days ahead,
And see her might and granite wonders there,
Beneath the touch of Time's unerring hand,
Like priceless treasures sinking in the sand.

THE TROPICS IN NEW YORK

Bananas ripe and green, and ginger-root
    Cocoa in pods and alligator pears,
And tangerines and mangoes and grape fruit,
    Fit for the highest prize at parish fairs,

Set in the window, bringing memories
    Of fruit-trees laden by low-singing rills,

---

*Almost all the poems in *Spring in New Hampshire and Other Poems* were included in *Harlem Shadows*. The poems here are in the same order as they appeared in *Harlem Shadows*. For poems originally published in periodicals, please refer to the Contents (pp. iii–v) of this volume for publication data.

30

And dewy dawns, and mystical blue skies
  In benediction over nun-like hills.

My eyes drew dim, and I could no more gaze;
  A wave of longing through my body swept,
And, hungry for the old, familiar ways,
  I turned aside and bowed my head and wept.

FLAME-HEART

So much I have forgotten in ten years,
So much in ten brief years! I have forgot
What time the purple apples come to juice,
And what month brings the shy forget-me-not.
I have forgot the special, startling season
Of the pimento's flowering and fruiting;
What time of year the ground doves brown the fields
And fill the noonday with their curious fluting.
I have forgotten much, but still remember
The poinsettia's red, blood-red, in warm December.

I still recall the honey-fever grass,
But cannot recollect the high days when
We rooted them out of the ping-wing path
To stop the mad bees in the rabbit pen.
I often try to think in what sweet month
The languid painted ladies used to dapple
The yellow by-road mazing from the main,
Sweet with the golden threads of the rose-apple.
I have forgotten—strange—but quite remember
The poinsettia's red, blood-red, in warm December.

What weeks, what months, what time of the mild year
We cheated school to have our fling at tops?
What days our wine-thrilled bodies pulsed with joy
Feasting upon blackberries in the copse?
Oh some I know! I have embalmed the days,
Even the sacred moments when we played,
All innocent of passion, uncorrupt,
At noon and evening in the flame-heart's shade.
We were so happy, happy, I remember,
Beneath the poinsettia's red in warm December.

HOME THOUGHTS

Oh something just now must be happening there!
That suddenly and quiveringly here,
Amid the city's noises, I must think
Of mangoes leaning to the river's brink,
And dexterous Davie climbing high above,
The gold fruits ebon-speckled to remove,
And toss them quickly in the tangled mass
Of wis-wis twisted round the guinea grass.
And Cyril coming through the bramble-track
A prize bunch of bananas on his back;
And Georgie—none could ever dive like him—
Throwing his scanty clothes off for a swim;
And schoolboys, from Bridge-tunnel going home,
Watching the waters downward dash and foam.
This is no daytime dream, there's something in it,
Oh something's happening there this very minute!

ON BROADWAY

About me young and careless feet
Linger along the garish street;
    Above, a hundred shouting signs
Shed down their bright fantastic glow
    Upon the merry crowd and lines
Of moving carriages below.
Oh wonderful is Broadway—only
My heart, my heart is lonely.

Desire naked, linked with Passion,
Goes strutting by in brazen fashion;
    From playhouse, cabaret and inn
The rainbow lights of Broadway blaze
    All gay without, all glad within.
As in a dream I stand and gaze
At Broadway, shining Broadway—only
My heart, my heart is lonely.

THE BARRIER

I must not gaze at them although
Your eyes are dawning day;
I must not watch you as you go
Your sun-illumined way.

I hear but I must never heed
The fascinating note,
Which, fluting like a river reed,
Comes from your trembling throat.

I must not see upon your face
Love's softly glowing spark;
For there's the barrier of race,
You're fair and I am dark.

NORTH AND SOUTH

O sweet are tropic lands for waking dreams!
  There time and life move lazily along.
There by the banks of blue and silver streams
  Grass-sheltered crickets chirp incessant song;
Gay-colored lizards loll all through the day,
  Their tongues outstretched for careless little flies.

And swarthy children in the fields at play,
  Look upward, laughing at the smiling skies.
A breath of idleness is in the air
  That casts a subtle spell upon all things,
And love and mating-time are everywhere,
  And wonder to life's commonplaces clings.

The fluttering humming-bird darts through the trees,
  And dips his long beak in the big bell-flowers.
The leisured buzzard floats upon the breeze,
  Riding a crescent cloud for endless hours.
The sea beats softly on the emerald strands—
  O sweet for quiet dreams are tropic lands!

AFTER THE WINTER

Some day, when trees have shed their leaves
    And against the morning's white
The shivering birds beneath the eaves
    Have sheltered for the night,
We'll turn our faces southward, love,
    Toward the summer isle
Where bamboos spire the shafted grove
    And wide-mouthed orchids smile.

And we will seek the quiet hill
    Where towers the cotton tree,
And leaps the laughing crystal rill,
    And works the droning bee.
And we will build a cottage there
    Beside an open glade,
With black-ribbed blue-bells blowing near,
    And ferns that never fade.

HARLEM SHADOWS

I hear the halting footsteps of a lass
    In Negro Harlem when the night lets fall
Its veil. I see the shapes of girls who pass
    To bend and barter at desire's call.
Ah, little dark girls who in slippered feet
Go prowling through the night from street to street!

Through the long night until the silver break
    Of day the little gray feet know no rest;
Through the lone night until the last snow-flake
    Has dropped from heaven upon the earth's
        white breast,
The dusky, half-clad girls of tired feet
Are trudging, thinly shod, from street to street.

Ah, stern harsh world, that in the wretched way
    Of poverty, dishonor and disgrace,
Has pushed the timid little feet of clay,
    The sacred brown feet of my fallen race!
Ah, heart of me, the weary, weary feet
In Harlem wandering from street to street.

THE WHITE CITY

I will not toy with it nor bend an inch.
Deep in the secret chambers of my heart
I muse my life-long hate, and without flinch
I bear it nobly as I live my part.
My being would be a skeleton, a shell,
If this dark Passion that fills my every mood,
And makes my heaven in the white world's hell,
Did not forever feed me vital blood.
I see the mighty city through a mist—
The strident trains that speed the goaded mass,
The poles and spires and towers vapor-kissed,
The fortressed port through which the great ships pass,
The tides, the wharves, the dens I contemplate,
Are sweet like wanton loves because I hate.

MY MOTHER

Reg wished me to go with him to the field;
I paused because I did not want to go,
But in her quiet way she made me yield
Reluctantly,—for she was breathing low.
Her hand she slowly lifted from her lap
And, smiling sadly in the old sweet way,
She pointed to the nail where hung my cap;
Her eyes said: I shall last another day.
But scarcely had we reached the distant place
When o'er the hills we heard a faint bell ringing,
A boy came running up with frightened face,
We knew the fatal news that he was bringing:
I heard him listlessly and made no moan,
Although the only one I loved was gone.

The dawn departs, the morning is begun,
The trades come whispering from off the seas,
The fields of corn are golden in the sun,
The dark-brown tassels fluttering in the breeze.
The bell is sounding and the children pass,
Frog-leaping, skipping, shouting, laughing shrill,
Down the red road, over the pasture-grass,
Up to the school-house crumbling on the hill.

The older folk are at their peaceful toil,
Some pulling up the weeds, some plucking corn,
And others breaking up the sun-baked soil.
Float, faintly-scented breeze, at early morn
Over the earth, where mortals sow and reap.
Beneath its breast my mother lies asleep.

IN BONDAGE

I would be wandering in distant fields ·
Where man, and bird, and beast, lives leisurely,
And the old earth is kind, and ever yields
Her goodly gifts to all her children free;
Where life is fairer, lighter, less demanding,
And boys and girls have time and space for play
Before they come to years of understanding—
Somewhere I would be singing, far away.
For life is greater than the thousand wars
Men wage for it in their insatiate lust,
And will remain like the eternal stars,
When all that shines to-day is drift and dust.

But I am bound with you in your mean graves,
O black men, simple slaves of ruthless slaves.

HERITAGE

Now the dead past seems vividly alive,
    And in this shining moment I can trace,
Down through the vista of the vanished years,
    Your faun-like form, your fond elusive face.

And suddenly some secret spring's released,
    And unawares a riddle is revealed,
And I can read like large, black-lettered print,
    What seemed before a thing forever sealed.

I know the magic word, the graceful thought,
    The song that fills me in my lucid hours,

The spirit's wine that thrills my body through,
    And makes me music-drunk, are yours, all yours.

I cannot praise, for you have passed from praise,
    I have no tinted thought to paint you true;
But I can feel and I can write the word:
    The best of me is but the least of you.

WHEN I HAVE PASSED AWAY

When I have passed away and am forgotten,
    And no one living can recall my face,
When under alien sod my bones lie rotten
    With not a tree or stone to mark the place;

Perchance a pensive youth, with passion burning,
    For olden verse that smacks of love and wine,
The musty pages of old volumes turning,
    May light upon a little song of mine,

And he may softly hum the tune and wonder
    Who wrote the verses in the long ago;
Or he may sit him down awhile to ponder
    Upon the simple words that touch him so.

ENSLAVED

Oh when I think of my long-suffering race,
    For weary centuries, despised, oppressed
Enslaved and lynched, denied a human place
    In the great life line of the Christian West;
And in the Black Land disinherited,
    Robbed in the ancient country of its birth,
My heart grows sick with hate, becomes as lead,
    For this my race that has no home on earth.
Then from the dark depth of my soul I cry
    To the avenging angel to consume
The white man's world of wonders utterly:
    Let it be swallowed up in the earth's vast womb,
Or upward roll as sacrificial smoke
    To liberate my people from its yoke!

WINTER IN THE COUNTRY

Sweet Life! how lovely to be here
    And feel the soft sea-laden breeze
Strike my flushed face, the spruce's fair
    Free limbs to see, the lesser trees'

Bare hands to touch, the sparrow's cheep
    To heed, and watch his nimble flight
Above the short brown grass asleep.
    Love glorious in his friendly might,

Music that every heart could bless,
    And thoughts of life serene, divine,
Beyond my power to express,
    Crown round this lifted heart of mine!

But oh! to leave this paradise
    For the city's dirty basement room,
Where, beauty hidden from the eyes,
    A table, bed, bureau and broom

In corner set, two crippled chairs
    All covered up with dust and grim
With hideousness and scars of years,
    And gaslight burning weird and dim,

Will welcome me . . . And yet, and yet
    This very wind, the winter birds,
The glory of the soft sunset,
    Come there to me in words.

SPRING IN NEW HAMPSHIRE

(TO J. L. J. F. E.)

Too green the springing April grass,
    Too blue the silver-speckled sky,
For me to linger here, alas,
    While happy winds go laughing by,
Wasting the golden hours indoors,
Washing windows and scrubbing floors.

Too wonderful the April night,
    Too faintly sweet the first May flowers,

The stars too gloriously bright,
    For me to spend the evening hours,
When fields are fresh and streams are leaping,
Wearied, exhausted, dully sleeping.

ON THE ROAD

Roar of the rushing train fearfully rocking,
Impatient people jammed in line for food,
The rasping noise of cars together knocking,
And worried waiters, some in ugly mood,
Crowding into the choking pantry hole
To call out dishes for each angry glutton
Exasperated grown beyond control,
From waiting for his soup or fish or mutton.
At last the station's reached, the engine stops;
For bags and wraps the red-caps circle round;
From off the step the passenger lightly hops,
And seeks his cab or tram-car homeward bound;
The waiters pass out weary, listless, glum,
To spend their tips on harlots, cards and rum.

THE HARLEM DANCER

Applauding youths laughed with young prostitutes
And watched her perfect, half-clothed body sway;
Her voice was like the sound of blended flutes
Blown by black players upon a picnic day.
She sang and danced on gracefully and calm,
The light gauze hanging loose about her form;
To me she seemed a proudly-swaying palm
Grown lovelier for passing through a storm.
Upon her swarthy neck black shiny curls
Luxuriant fell; and tossing coins in praise,
The wine-flushed, bold-eyed boys, and even the girls,
Devoured her shape with eager, passionate gaze;
But looking at her falsely-smiling face,
I knew her self was not in that strange place.

THE TIRED WORKER

O whisper, O my soul! The afternoon
Is waning into evening, whisper soft!
Peace, O my rebel heart! for soon the moon
From out its misty veil will swing aloft!
Be patient, weary body, soon the night
Will wrap thee gently in her sable sheet,
And with a leaden sigh thou wilt invite
To rest thy tired hands and aching feet.
The wretched day was theirs, the night is mine;
Come tender sleep, and fold me to thy breast.
But what steals out the gray clouds red like wine?
O dawn! O dreaded dawn! O let me rest
Weary my veins, my brain, my life! Have pity!
No! Once again the harsh, the ugly city.

OUTCAST

For the dim regions whence my fathers came
My spirit, bondaged by the body, longs.
Words felt, but never heard, my lips would frame;
My soul would sing forgotten jungle songs.
I would go back to darkness and to peace,
But the great western world holds me in fee,
And I may never hope for full release
While to its alien gods I bend my knee.
Something in me is lost, forever lost,
Some vital thing has gone out of my heart,
And I must walk the way of life a ghost
Among the sons of earth, a thing apart;
For I was born, far from my native clime,
Under the white man's menace, out of time.

I KNOW MY SOUL

I plucked my soul out of its secret place,
And held it to the mirror of my eye,
To see it like a star against the sky,

A twitching body quivering in space,
A spark of passion shining on my face.
And I explored it to determine why
This awful key to my infinity
Conspires to rob me of sweet joy and grace.
And if the sign may not be fully read,
If I can comprehend but not control,
I need not gloom my days with futile dread,
Because I see a part and not the whole.
Contemplating the strange, I'm comforted
By this narcotic thought: I know my soul.

BIRDS OF PREY

Their shadow dims the sunshine of our day,
As they go lumbering across the sky,
Squawking in joy of feeling safe on high,
Beating their heavy wings of owlish gray.
They scare the singing birds of earth away
As, greed-impelled, they circle threateningly,
Watching the toilers with malignant eye,
From their exclusive haven—birds of prey.
They swoop down for the spoil in certain might,
And fasten in our bleeding flesh their claws.
They beat us to surrender weak with fright,
And tugging and tearing without let or pause,
They flap their hideous wings in grim delight,
And stuff our gory hearts into their maws.

EXHORTATION: SUMMER, 1919

Through the pregnant universe rumbles life's terrific thunder,
    And Earth's bowels quake with terror; strange and terrible
        storms break,
Lightning-torches flame the heavens, kindling souls of men,
        thereunder:
    Africa! long ages sleeping, O my motherland, awake!

In the East the clouds glow crimson with the new dawn that
        is breaking,

And its golden glory fills the western skies.
O my brothers and my sisters, wake! arise!
For the new birth rends the old earth and the very dead
     are waking,
  Ghosts are turned flesh, throwing off the grave's disguise,
  And the foolish, even children, are made wise;
For the big earth groans in travail for the strong, new world
     in making—
  O my brothers, dreaming for dim centuries,
  Wake from sleeping; to the East turn, turn your eyes!

Oh the night is sweet for sleeping, but the shining day's
     for working;
  Sons of the seductive night, for your children's
    children's sake,
From the deep primeval forests where the crouching
     leopard's lurking,
  Lift your heavy-lidded eyes, Ethiopia! awake!

In the East the clouds glow crimson with the new dawn
    that is breaking,
  And its golden glory fills the western skies.
  O my brothers and my sisters, wake! arise!
For the new birth rends the old earth and the very dead
     are waking,
  Ghosts are turned flesh, throwing off the grave's disguise,
  And the foolish, even children, are made wise;
For the big earth groans in travail for the strong,
     new world in making—
  O my brothers, dreaming for long centuries,
  Wake from sleeping; to the East turn, turn your eyes!

BAPTISM

Into the furnace let me go alone;
Stay you without in terror of the heat.
I will go naked in—for thus 'tis sweet—
Into the weird depths of the hottest zone.
I will not quiver in the frailest bone,
You will not note a flicker of defeat;
My heart shall tremble not its fate to meet,
My mouth give utterance to any moan.
The yawning oven spits forth fiery spears;

Red aspish tongues shout wordlessly my name.
Desire destroys, consumes my mortal fears,
Transforming me into a shape of flame.
I will come out, back to your world of tears,
A stronger soul within a finer frame.

IF WE MUST DIE

If we must die, let it not be like hogs
Hunted and penned in an inglorious spot,
While round us bark the mad and hungry dogs,
Making their mock at our accursed lot.
If we must die, O let us nobly die,
So that our precious blood may not be shed
In vain; then even the monsters we defy
Shall be constrained to honor us though dead!
O kinsmen! we must meet the common foe!
Though far outnumbered let us show us brave,
And for their thousand blows deal one deathblow!
What though before us lies the open grave?
Like men we'll face the murderous, cowardly pack,
Pressed to the wall, dying, but fighting back!

SUBWAY WIND

Far down, down through the city's great gaunt gut
    The gray train rushing bears the weary wind;
In the packed cars the fans the crowd's breath cut,
    Leaving the sick and heavy air behind.
And pale-cheeked children seek the upper door
    To give their summer jackets to the breeze;
Their laugh is swallowed in the deafening roar
    Of captive wind that moans for fields and seas;
Seas cooling warm where native schooners drift
    Through sleepy waters, while gulls wheel and sweep,
Waiting for windy waves the keels to lift
    Lightly among the islands of the deep;
Islands of lofty palm trees blooming white
    That lend their perfume to the tropic sea,
Where fields lie idle in the dew-drenched night,
    And the Trades float above them fresh and free.

POETRY

Sometimes I tremble like a storm-swept flower,
And seek to hide my tortured soul from thee,
Bowing my head in deep humility
Before the silent thunder of thy power.
Sometimes I flee before thy blazing light,
As from the specter of pursuing death;
Intimidated lest thy mighty breath,
Windways, will sweep me into utter night.
For oh, I fear they will be swallowed up—
The loves which are to me of vital worth,
My passion and my pleasure in the earth—
And lost forever in thy magic cup!
I fear, I fear my truly human heart
Will perish on the altar-stone of art!

A PRAYER

'Mid the discordant noises of the day I hear thee calling;
I stumble as I fare along Earth's way; keep me from falling.

Mine eyes are open but they cannot see for gloom of night;
I can no more than lift my heart to thee for inward light.

The wild and fiery passion of my youth consumes my soul;
In agony I turn to thee for truth and self-control.

For Passion and all the pleasures it can give will die the death;
But this of me eternally must live, thy borrowed breath.

'Mid the discordant noises of the day I hear thee calling;
I stumble as I fare along Earth's way; keep me from falling.

WHEN DAWN COMES TO THE CITY

The tired cars go grumbling by,
    The moaning, groaning cars,
And the old milk-carts go rumbling by
    Under the same dull stars.
Out of the tenements, cold as stone,

Dark figures start for work;
I watch them sadly shuffle on,
'Tis dawn, dawn in New York.

But I would be on the island of the sea,
In the heart of the island of the sea,
Where the cocks are crowing, crowing, crowing,
And the hens are cackling in the rose-apple tree,
Where the old draft-horse is neighing, neighing, neighing
Out on the brown dew-silvered lawn,
And the tethered cow is lowing, lowing, lowing,
And dear old Ned is braying, braying, braying,
And the shaggy Nannie goat is calling, calling, calling
From her little trampled corner of the long wide lea
That stretches to the waters of the hill-stream falling
Sheer upon the flat rocks joyously!
There, oh there! on the island of the sea
There I would be at dawn.

The tired cars go grumbling by,
The crazy, lazy cars,
And the same milk-carts go rumbling by
Under the dying stars.
A lonely newsboy hurries by,
Humming a recent ditty;
Red streaks strike through the gray of the sky,
The dawn comes to the city.

But I would be on the island of the sea,
In the heart of the island of the sea,
Where the cocks are crowing, crowing, crowing,
And the hens are cackling in the rose-apple tree,
Where the old draft-horse is neighing, neighing, neighing
Out on the brown dew-silvered lawn,
And the tethered cow is lowing, lowing, lowing,
And dear old Ned is braying, braying, braying,
And the shaggy Nannie goat is calling, calling, calling
From her little trampled corner of the long wide lea
That stretches to the waters of the hill-stream falling
Sheer upon the flat rocks joyously!
There, oh there! on the island of the sea
There I would be at dawn.

O WORD I LOVE TO SING

O word I love to sing! thou art too tender
   For all the passions agitating me;
For all my bitterness thou art too tender,
   I cannot pour my red soul into thee.

O haunting melody! thou art too slender,
   Too fragile like a globe of crystal glass;
For all my stormy thoughts thou art too slender,
   The burden from my bosom will not pass.

O tender word! O melody so slender!
   O tears of passion saturate with brine,
O words, unwilling words, ye can not render
   My hatred for the foe of me and mine.

SUMMER MORN IN NEW HAMPSHIRE

All yesterday it poured, and all night long
   I could not sleep; the rain unceasing beat
Upon the shingled roof like a weird song,
   Upon the grass like running children's feet.
And down the mountains by the dark cloud kissed,
   Like a strange shape in filmy veiling dressed,
Slid slowly, silently, the wraith-like mist,
   And nestled soft against the earth's wet breast.

But lo, there was a miracle at dawn!
   The still air stirred at touch of the faint breeze,
The sun a sheet of gold bequeathed the lawn,
   The songsters twittered in the rustling trees.
And all things were transfigured in the day,
   But me whom radiant beauty could not move;
For you, more wonderful, were far away,
   And I was blind with hunger for your love.

ROMANCE

To clasp you now and feel your head close-pressed,
Scented and warm against my beating breast;

To whisper soft and quivering your name,
And drink the passion burning in your frame;

To lie at full length, taut, with cheek to cheek,
And tease your mouth with kisses till you speak

Love words, mad words, dream words, sweet senseless words,
Melodious like notes of mating birds;

To hear you ask if I shall love always,
And myself answer: Till the end of days;

To feel your easeful sigh of happiness
When on your trembling lips I murmur: Yes;

It is so sweet. We know it is not true.
What matters it? The night must shed her dew.

We know it is not true, but it is sweet—
The poem with this music is complete.

FLOWER OF LOVE

The perfume of your body dulls my sense.
   I want nor wine nor weed; your breath alone
Suffices. In this moment rare and tense
   I worship at your breast. The flower is blown,
The saffron petals tempt my amorous mouth,
   The yellow heart is radiant now with dew
Soft-scented, redolent of my loved South;
   O flower of love! I give myself to you.
Uncovered on your couch of figured green,
   Here let us linger indivisible.
The portals of your sanctuary unseen
   Receive my offering, yielding unto me.
Oh, with our love the night is warm and deep!
   The air is sweet, my flower, and sweet the flute
Whose music lulls our burning brain to sleep,
   While we lie loving, passionate and mute.

A MEMORY OF JUNE

When June comes dancing on the death of May,
   With scarlet roses tinting her green breast,
And mating thrushes ushering in her day,
   And Earth on tiptoe for her golden guest,

I always see the evening when we met—
  The first of June baptized in tender rain—
And walked home through the wide streets, gleaming wet,
  Arms locked, our warm flesh pulsing with love's pain.

I always see the cheerful little room,
  And in the corner, fresh and white, the bed,
Sweet scented with a delicate perfume,
  Wherein for one night only we were wed;

Where in the starlit stillness we lay mute,
  And heard the whispering showers all night long,
And your brown burning body was a lute
  Whereon my passion played his fevered song.

When June comes dancing on the death of May,
  With scarlet roses staining her fair feet,
My soul takes leave of me to sing all day
  A love so fugitive and so complete.

ONE YEAR AFTER

I.

Not once in all our days of poignant love,
Did I a single instant give to thee
My undivided being wholly free.
Not all thy potent passion could remove
The barrier that loomed between to prove
The full supreme surrendering of me.
Oh, I was beaten, helpless utterly
Against the shadow-fact with which I strove.
For when a cruel power forced me to face
The truth which poisoned our illicit wine,
That even I was faithless to my race
Bleeding beneath the iron hand of thine,
Our union seemed a monstrous thing and base!
I was an outcast from thy world and mine.

II.

Adventure-seasoned and storm-buffeted,
I shun all signs of anchorage, because

The zest of life exceeds the bound of laws.
New gales of tropic fury round my head
Break lashing me through hours of soulful dread;
But when the terror thins and, spent, withdraws,
Leaving me wondering awhile, I pause—
But soon again the risky ways I tread!
No rigid road for me, no peace, no rest,
While molten elements run through my blood;
And beauty-burning bodies manifest
Their warm, heart-melting motions to be wooed;
And passion boldly rising in my breast,
Like rivers of the Spring, lets loose its flood.

JASMINES

Your scent is in the room.
Swiftly it overwhelms and conquers me!
Jasmines, night jasmines, perfect of perfume,
Heavy with dew before the dawn of day!
Your face was in the mirror. I could see
You smile and vanish suddenly away,
Leaving behind the vestige of a tear.
Sad suffering face, from parting grown so dear!
Night jasmine cannot bloom in this cold place;
Without the street is wet and weird with snow;
The cold nude trees are tossing to and fro;
Too stormy is the night for your fond face;
For your low voice too loud the wind's mad roar.
But oh, your scent—jasmines, jasmines that grow
Luxuriant, clustered round your cottage door!

MEMORIAL

Your body was a sacred cell always,
    A jewel that grew dull in garish light,
An opal which beneath my wondering gaze
    Gleamed rarely, softly throbbing in the night.

I touched your flesh with reverential hands,
    For you were sweet and timid like a flower

That blossoms out of barren tropic sands,
   Shedding its perfume in one golden hour.

You yielded to my touch with gentle grace,
   And though my passion was a mighty wave
That buried you beneath its strong embrace,
   You were yet happy in the moment's grave.

Still more than passion consummate to me,
   More than the nuptials immemorial sung,
Was the warm thrill that melted me to see
   Your clean brown body, beautiful and young;

The joy in your maturity at length,
   The peace that filled my soul like cooling wine,
When you responded to my tender strength,
   And pressed your heart exulting into mine.

How shall I with such memories of you
   In coarser forms of love fruition find?
No, I would rather like a ghost pursue
   The fairy phantoms of my lonely mind.

THIRST

My spirit wails for water, water now!
My tongue is aching dry, my throat is hot
For water, fresh rain shaken from a bough,
Or dawn dews heavy in some leafy spot.
My hungry body's burning for a swim
In sunlit water where the air is cool,
As in Trout Valley where upon a limb
The golden finch sings sweetly to the pool.
Oh water, water, when the night is done,
When day steals gray-white through the window-pane,
Clear silver water when I wake, alone,
All impotent of parts, of fevered brain;
Pure water from a forest fountain first,
To wash me, cleanse me, and to quench my thirst!

Index of Titles